Copyright © Suzannah Showler, 2014
Published by ECW Press
2120 Queen Street East, Suite 200
Toronto, Ontario, Canada M4E 1E2
416-694-3348 / info@ecwpress.com

All rights reserved. No part of this publication may be reproduced, stored in a retrieval system, or transmitted in any form by any process — electronic, mechanical, photocopying, recording, or otherwise — without the prior written permission of the copyright owners and ECW Press. The scanning, uploading, and distribution of this book via the Internet or via any other means without the permission of the publisher is illegal and punishable by law. Please purchase only authorized electronic editions, and do not participate in or encourage electronic piracy of copyrighted materials. Your support of the author's rights is appreciated.

Library and Archives Canada Cataloguing in Publication

Showler, Suzannah, author
Failure to thrive / Suzannah Showler.

Poems.
Issued in print and electronic formats.
ISBN 978-1-77041-202-6 (PBK)
978-1-77090-531-3 (EPUB)
978-1-77090-530-6 (PDF)

I. Title.

PS8637.H69F33 2014   C811'.6
                C2013-908020-1
                C2013-908021-X

Editor for the press: Michael Holmes
Cover design: Natalie Olsen
Author photo: Stephanie Coffey
    (stephaniecoffeyphotography.com)
Type: Rachel Ironstone
Printing: Coach House   1 2 3 4 5

 MISFIT

 Get the eBook free! Purchase the print edition and receive the eBook free! For details, go to ecwpress.com/eBook.

The publication of *Failure to Thrive* has been generously supported by the Canada Council for the Arts which last year invested $157 million to bring the arts to Canadians throughout the country, and by the Ontario Arts Council (OAC), an agency of the Government of Ontario, which last year funded 1,681 individual artists and 1,125 organizations in 216 communities across Ontario for a total of $52.8 million. We also acknowledge the financial support of the Government of Canada through the Canada Book Fund for our publishing activities, and the contribution of the Government of Ontario through the Ontario Book Publishing Tax Credit and the Ontario Media Development Corporation.

Printed and bound in Canada

POEMS
SUZANNAH SHOWLER
ecw press | a misFit book

CONTENTS

SENSORY ANCHORS

The Reason | 3
Notes Towards Something Nearly Allegorical | 4
Day for Evasion | 5
Notes on Integrity | 6
Crossing the High Level Bridge | 7
Jeopardy | 8
Remote Sharing | 9
Thirteen Subcategories | 10
Pretty Good Time at the Olfactory Factory | 11
You and Your Rich Inner Life | 12
Offer | 13

MUSEUM MOUTH

Sucks to Be You and Other True Taunts | 17
    i) I Know You Are, But What Am I?
    ii) Why Don't You Go Home and Cry About It?
    iii) Takes One to Know One
    iv) Stop Hitting Yourself
    v) Do You Have a Staring Problem?
Already Today You Have Had Several Very Good
    Ideas | 22

WHAT YOU SEE IS WHAT YOU GET

Flare | 35
Portraits of Several Lamps Broken
    While House-Sitting | 36
I Wish You Luck and Prosperity! | 38
The Windsor Asylum | 40
Whale Fall | 41
A Short History of the Visible | 43

SOME CRUCIAL ELEMENT
A Short and Useful Guide
   to Living in the World | 55
Seasonal Goods | 57
Bracketing Paradox | 59
Fun with Counterfactual Conditionals! | 60
Position: Monster | 62
Notes Towards Something
   Nearly Allegorical Also | 63
Confessions from the Driver
   of the Google Street View Car | 64
Change of State | 66
Rapture Begets Sweater Begets Rapture | 67

KEEN FREQUENCIES
I Liked the Part Where | 73
Dread for Something Useful | 75
Some Final Explanatory Thoughts | 77
Keep Scrolling | 79
Good Thing | 80
One Possible Explanation
   for What Appears to Be the Case | 82

Notes on the Poems || 85
Acknowledgements || 87

SENSORY ANCHORS

THE REASON

Because you are the kind of person who
lets their perishables expire the way they want to,
from the inside out (say, like an eggplant,
the colour velour was invented to live up to,
rubber-skinned, preserving its opaque dignity
until the eleventh hour when you touch it with,
maybe, a dirty chopstick, and it collapses
into its own long-sludge-gone guts),
the kind of person whose circadian rhythm
has a half-life, who has too-vividly imagined
the texture of wet rat fur (considered the rat
as what might emerge, grease-licked, from the turnpike
of the throat), who worries over a receding gumline,
spends mornings after-punched from blown-out
night hues (colour-blocked, full-field-of-view,
edges like scintillating scotomas), keeps the moths
in the pantry for pets, has a mantra ("there is too much
of everything") to scrawl across
any surface that will end (humid water-film
on windows, Post-its laid out in art supply stores
to test the mettle of pens) —

I know you will know what I mean when I say:

Vacuum me up. Blot my face out with a plunger.
Let my mitosis be reverse-engineered.
Withdraw me into the dark.

I take it all back.

NOTES TOWARDS SOMETHING NEARLY ALLEGORICAL

The ground, clay heavy, follows you across the field,
caught in your tread, grey and mottled with the aftermath of a hobby harvest:
the stalks of sunflowers mummified, light as bird bones.

You arrive at the back of the property, your feet scraped equine
on the unmowed grass behind the house. There is the house again
in miniature, in stone, and you go into it.

In a room freshly turned into a shrine,
you reach into the viscera of a dust green duffel,
pass your hand over.

When you leave, you'll pull yourself out of the valley
to the tune of a few hours' hitchhike,
moving with an odd-digited limp, carried
onward by the skin of your thumbs.

DAY FOR EVASION

The morning offers evidence of a rain you slept through,
pavement like grease soaked through a sandwich bag,

and there's definitely a fire burning inside the metal Muppet-mouthed
industrial garbage bin open outside No Frills. The fire's low and mangy,

like a nest where light hatches, and the air out here
smells like a dentist's office in its busy time: overheating rubber,

periodic elements, a fresh mess of fragile membrane
cut into, pulled back — every hard, impacted thing removed.

This is a pretty good day for evasion, and you'd like to
volunteer your service for something clean and memorable,

maybe running interference for the No Frills shoppers tenderly
nosing their way past displays shocking as capped front teeth,

performing what reads as a well-considered dumb show. This course
of action has all the vision, all the hoist of a boom lift. Now seems

as good a time as any to admit: you've never seen something so thoroughly
as to forget its name, and more than once, the constellations have let you down.

You can feel the day's details waiting to pitch towards you like an airbag
deploying an ultra-white, full-frontal bloom of goodness in your face.

The fire in the bin is still brooding.
You'd like to tell someone its meaning isn't lost on you.

NOTES ON INTEGRITY

What if we stopped predicting the weather
and agreed to run it ragged?

To demonstrate: a dramatization
of a pigeon being hit by a car, except in this

instance, the pigeon wins. Once a month
it's moving day. Walking home, you'll notice

everyone is having a night in their lives.
Most people are now experts on design.

I'm pretty sure this guy I know is faking
imposter syndrome. But don't we all

just want to stand, mostly upright,
in a stick figure forest of contemporaries?

At the very least, I'd like to make a name
for myself in the lost art of skywriting.

I was going to say something crucial.
But I forget what.

CROSSING THE HIGH LEVEL BRIDGE

A seagull jumps off, the wind cracks it open over the nestled knot
of some inner-bird hinge like the ugly joisting of a jaw,

and it's cradled, portside to your cheek, carving out the pendulum
of a weight even-keeling from a mobile short on slack.

If this day's hours are a page, then minutes find their end in folded birds,
and your relationship to passing time is best described as vigilant: you're careful

with wings, the sharp-cornered pleats that make a beak, aware that in your hands
you're holding paper's best impression of a weapon.

The bridge is very long.
The wind pushes you in some direction.

And that damn seagull hangs in a new plane of gravity it's been gifted,
waiting for nothing, comforted by its new and enviable way of being alone.

JEOPARDY

What is the Magna Carta?
Who is Helen Keller?
What are light emitting diodes?
Where is West Texas?

What is a carbuncle?
What is fractional distillation?
What are and, or, nor, for, yet, but, and so?
Who is Genghis Khan?

Where is the abyssal zone?
What is a hypnic jerk?
What is elbow grease?

Where are the blind leading the blind?
What is a dissociative fugue?
What is a proof of purchase?
Where is the last place you would think to look?

What are the contents of your refrigerator?
What is a state of exception?
What is an organ-bruising punch to the gut?

Who is the patron saint of misdirected feelings?
What is the etymology of disappointment?
Where is the origin of the problem?
What is authentic evidence of some unlikely thing?

What is nostalgia for something that never occurred?
Where is the best place to hide evidence of wrongdoing?
What is the direction in which we are currently headed?

REMOTE SHARING

One day you wake up, and it's like
you've already been to Tuscaloosa,

passed the taxidermist's licensing
exam, and now you're roving the low

country in a PT Cruiser, ego
bloating like a sourdough starter.

The truth is the turning radius
on this model is shit. The psychic

diagnosed your penchant for higher
learning, advised you tend your dream

diary with thinning shears, accept
every discarded cell phone ring

still branded on your nerves as a talisman.
Superstition has often come at you

with an orbit-dragging lust, but these
days you could probably make it

through hurricane season without
lamenting your disbanded trivia team.

THIRTEEN SUBCATEGORIES

found poem

Accidental deaths by location
Victims of aviation accidents or incidents
Accidental deaths by electrocution
Accidental deaths from falls
Filmed accidental deaths
Firearm accident victims
Deaths by horse-riding accident
Hunting accident deaths
Industrial accident deaths
People who died in ATV accidents
Railroad accident victims
Space program fatalities
Deaths in sport

PRETTY GOOD TIME AT THE OLFACTORY FACTORY

Human skull preserved
behind the bar in the officer's mess
at the local armoury.

Beach barbecue at low tide
on the outskirts of a mid-sized city
still flanked by industry.

Cabbage sliced late at night
with a steel knife.

Coconut-sweet wind laced with salt
bending around the near-albino mesa
of potash burped up out of the prairie.

Mildew-wet, Play-Dohy renovations
to the basement of a fixer-upper.

A Scratch 'n Sniff sticker
with all the good stuff
scratched out of it.

Bike lock in winter coaxed open
with a crème brûlée torch.

A flexible grade of rubber used
in the production of several toys
that were popular in the mid-nineties
and discontinued by the early aughts.

Sweat in a darkroom.

YOU AND YOUR RICH INNER LIFE

External conditions conspire to slip
along the waxy thread of your nerves

and hunker down, cathectic, in the carry-on
you keep at the ready for a flight

from the everyday. We sign off on an agreement
to accept what the senses offer: a volley of errors.

Anything to interrupt the hypnotic mumbling
that lips the inner retaining wall of the skull.

Nobody ever tells a stitch of metal vacuumed
inside a light bulb to conduct itself better.

The fear of letting too much wash past
without record is not unfounded.

It's never too late to change tack, drop
your sensory anchors elsewhere.

Your perceptions won't be watered down,
though you might still hold your digits

over a light source, feeling for residual heat,
and get nothing back. Too much light

will clear away the murk of shadow detail
complicating any record of the event.

Call this getting washed out. Don't forget:
exposure is something you can die of.

OFFER

Something that resembles a bird feeder,
but where each of the tiny shunts
that leaks out grain is equipped to handle
your whispering instead.

Or maybe more like:
A ball of wax, a candle, miniature rolling pin,
an instruction guide for preserving
uncomfortably shaped objects.

An index of useful hiding places.

Better yet, the mnemonic device
for remembering all your good qualities
that have been glimpsed
but not lived up to, like flash sightings
of cryptids that go unrecorded.

By which I really mean
the technology with which to record
unlikely events in the first place —
a surface proof can impress itself upon,
turn up like lines on an Etch A Sketch.

Now that I think about it,
I might have had it right the first time.

So think about my original offer.
When your spit-heavy thoughts
start to backwash, you could sit the thing
on your mantel like an urn or a portrait
of the presiding household god.

Or bring it to a crowd's inner sanctum.
String it up like a piñata.
Wait for the show.

MUSEUM MOUTH

SUCKS TO BE YOU AND OTHER TRUE TAUNTS

i) I Know You Are, But What Am I?

I have to say, these strangers form great
cognitive maps. There they go,
good and oriented, marking their way
from cheese shop to florist
and never once losing a stranglehold
on their rowed-up ducks, no matter
what they've seen coming or going.
They purchase whatever comes in
glass bottles, and sometimes, in the break
between adventures, there's spinning to do.
Look, I don't have a strand in this hairball,
and if I put something down on the odds
of things turning upright, I still feel it was
money well-waylaid. Next thing
you'll be asking how it is I sleep at night,
and the answer is the same as the answer
to most things: it's a trick of the light.

ii) Why Don't You Go Home and Cry About It?

I have a feeling about a very slow
apocalypse where we are all drawn
back to our hometowns by something
like a magnet that attracts whatever
inside us is most mediocre and true.
So, when the world begins to end,
if you have a minute, please promise
to tell me more about all the other
people you've fucked, how they
had skin almost too firm to register
touch, how their pussies were basically
luminescent, and, in particular, I'd like
to know in what order their clothes
came off when they undressed,
because I'll need something
to think about when I am caught,
post-apocalyptically, in Ottawa,
Ontario, the capital of Canada,
where my parents still live.

iii) Takes One to Know One

Just because you can't see the fingerling
moulds packed up my nostrils like espresso
grinds, or feel the dirt's mineral sweat haloed
around me like the cell-thin buffer between
a vacuum seal and its charge, doesn't mean
I'm not dead. If you've failed to bury me,
and the ants single-filing through my ear canal
are, as you say, all in the mind, that's a testament
only to your clumsiness with ceremony
and gardening tools. Am I cramping your style?
Paper looks so floppily harmless until you
turn it sideways. You've used this against me.
Let this be a reminder that the dead bleed, too,
and at greater personal expense. I don't know
why you're kicking up this fuss. I've only ever
haunted you in a quiet, mossy sort of way.

iv) Stop Hitting Yourself

No matter how many times you click
the Unsubscribe link, the newsletter still
finds you. You skim through it like
you're high-grading grapes out of
cantaloupe-heavy fruit salad. You can
never help yourself. Scroll back further:
at every phase in utero, you, too, were
compared to fruit. Very little of that
sympathy remains, though sometimes,
when the barometer hits a certain
mark, a touch of the old melon-ness
might still be felt in your joints. Better
posture is the first step in any self-
improvement program, and agency
is all about weight distribution.
Regret has a nasty habit of going
straight to the face.

v) Do You Have a Staring Problem?

The mould on the ceiling looks like a negative
image of a galaxy creeping its way into the future.
We're told stars do this, and we believe it
because the relationship between light and time
is one thing pretty much everyone agrees on.
If you're ever in space, reach into a shadow
deep enough and your arm will disappear
at the root. The mould never grows. Like strung-out
mulch at the bottom of a teacup, it will be read
as a flock taking off and hanging a louie in tandem,
which is what birds do to make humans feel badly
about our own ability to make group decisions.
Still, we have our moments: fitting together
Lego-sized sightlines into something we can
all take for granted, a vision too big to fail.
The sky has a ceiling, and after that you're in space.
From there, a man can fall the length of a protracted
guitar solo and wind up in the desert. Reach into
a shadow and go limbless. Stare down the limelight
of everything that hasn't happened, but will.

ALREADY TODAY YOU HAVE HAD SEVERAL VERY GOOD IDEAS

i)

I'm working on something
you could get away with.

Balm of platitudes,
frantic misdemeanours,
a collection of locks
that won't unclutch.

Spend an hour trying
to exercise remote control.

The plot of your life
dovetails with sweeps week.

ii)

Artificial lighting is the pits.

Singerie orchestra, lead-laced paint,
a bad case of museum mouth.

Punch a line like it's a predator.

All the better to see you with.

iii)

The notes are still there, but the tails
are getting shorter.

A balding spool of magnetic tape,
clear-minded projector beam
turning up dustless air,
sand magnified
to the power of whatever.

Sustains and decays
fall away from the back.

The thing is, we're building
on something here.

iv)

The crowd deplanes with next-generation
melancholy ruffled in.

Spanworm pitch limping fits,
patrol the air over sidewalks.

The street-level living room is often
mistaken for a beautiful objects shop.

Shoes twin-bobbing over telephone wires
don't represent anything.

You're welcome.

v)

Have I already told you this?

Double-jointed hinges flexed to forgive,
clapboard rough as a chest cough,
the romantic, open-ended names
of highways.

Pull at the hatch.

Empty out all your threats.

vi)

Is working online at home the new gold rush?

Time spent paying attention
to all the otherwise, braiding
a love of woe into it.

This is your calling card.

The world longs away like ice floes
pressing into territories
you'll never get a visa for.

So bud your ears shut and wait,
stopgapped, to incubate a new season's
better blooms. Spores in the chest.

You're making your own fun.

vii)

You've got a pretty good idea
of where this is going by now.

Fatty sheath, plenum of idling thoughts.

Making things fit together
isn't the hard part.

String a tooth up to the door
and slam something.

viii)

The film of resistance
you're wrapped up in:
it's mainly your own dead cells,
the stuff that turns up under your nails
after scratching at the remains
of wounds accrued or conjured.

Once you start in that way,
it's pretty hard to stop.

Better to just wait it out, look at things.
Like dirty snow cresting other snow,
to use a recent example.

ix)

Don't take this the wrong way.

Badly stuffed chair, jar of pennies,
temperamental radio left on.

A finger runs up a metal string.

x)

Already today you have had
several very good ideas.

Something good, something
better, something else.

You're standing still,
counting backwards by sevens.

I'm coming to you direct, by way
of this Rube Goldberg machine.

WHAT YOU SEE IS WHAT YOU GET

FLARE

Bengal light shot up, blue-beamed into all the nothing,
flung out like a limb in first morning's muscle-reach,
a precedent still being set.

This reminds us that there's mass in everything.
Even light's residue haunting your eyelids from the inside,
projected onto the flesh-stretch of holland blinds
you pull down to mark off the you from all the not-you.

And we could invent a kind of barium swallow for eyes:
some milk-thick light to funnel down the pupil's open drain.
Send an image to bobble through
the optic nerves like a sewer pill.

It wouldn't be an exact science, but the truth is
we have enough exactness already.
It's the general we're lacking.

Light is a great leveller. There isn't much contained
in the planes it touches that we haven't already guessed at.

You still haven't asked me what the Bengal light signals.
And I haven't told you because I'm still not sure.
But I know there's something coming.
There's something coming after this.

PORTRAITS OF SEVERAL LAMPS BROKEN WHILE HOUSE-SITTING

Think of the death portraits as still frames
from a reverse-motion video of each demise:
lamps coming upright like break-dancers
fighting gravity with core strength; fire-bits
leaping back into sockets to become unborn flame;
glass archipelagos sucked into Pangea.

The small one was vulnerable, its cord lounging
like an Achilles spine. Its base was banged to a kilter
and three bulbs replaced before it was done for good.

Here's the reedy green one — it dragged
too much electricity from the wall,
flamed out from the effort.
It was too good for this world.

The tallest and strongest went down inexplicably,
all alone. We suspect it made a sound
like the prehistoric hybrid that evolved into the horse.
The thick glass dome left a galaxy on the floor.

To take the last image, lard the fallen with flowers
and serve them up, tableaued among their loved ones:
the industrial-thick bookshelf,
the ladder leaning into it that won't bear weight,
the grey couch that can coax a nap out of anyone.
You may need to use props, pin parts together,
create an illusion of life.

(How many lamps had I already broken
the night you threw me over your shoulder?
The way the ground abandoned me felt reckless.
I told you how much I weighed,

offering evidence of something. Your hand
on my calf calibrated the unexpected balance
we'd become, pulling me towards earth.)

Remember the lamps when they were at their finest,
revealing whole rooms, clearing away shadows
accumulated in corners as though bred from spores,
a dark that catches the periphery, stretches
into masses hovering just outside the vision,
always on the verge of approaching.
Remember that the lamplight held these back.

I WISH YOU LUCK AND PROSPERITY!

Dear Friend,

This letter was born of the hand of a doctor of Dutch-Polynesian descent
who carried in his blood the ancient mysteries of the guild
that cajoled the guardians of Easter Island from unyielding stone.

You are holding a coiled-up shot of luck and prosperity
ready to launch at you like a spring snake from a nut can!

Within five days of receiving this letter,
you must send it on to five friends upon whose hand
the touch of bounty belongs, and within one week
you will be haunted by blessings more persistent
than a knife-seller earning a commission.

Here is definite proof:

Within four days of mailing his letters, Nevin learned
that he had been selected by a panel of qualified jurists
for a $1 million prize of no known origin or cause.
He relocated to an equatorial slap of land couched
in the bluest stretch of the Pacific and now lives out his leisure days
casting golf balls towards each cardinal direction in turn.

Marcy did not pass this letter on, and she suffered boils
that sprouted from beneath the banks of her fingernails
and spread to all she touched.
Her husband's infected testicles bolted into his abdomen
and have not since descended.

This letter has been around the world eleven times already!

Stay true to its instructions, and luck will stroke you as surely as a lonely widow strokes a cat.

Do not break the chain!

THE WINDSOR ASYLUM

Lowest was Jean's preternatural warble,
spate of notes carrying a regatta of old-world curses
that strained, wood-stained, to reach us.

From Gary it was a half-drugged gangling of cans
bagged with awkward slip knot persisting up
the aft chamber of stairs — the kind of resolve
applied to a plan not fully thought through.

Beneath us were Nancy's cats, beloved but near-feral,
multiplying seamlessly below the dysfunctional flue
of the fireplace.

And nestled among the doors opening onto nothing,
in the illogical teratoma of hallways,
our flat sat cradled as a sternum.

There is something there, still, in the unplanned
sounds that infected us: our tongues seizing like fish
skewered through the centre, a quick spasm of verbs.

We were sustained by this, marvelling,
knowing ourselves by what we weren't.
But we were in it: flaking aquamarine
unequal to the kinless cold.

The house set back from the street.

WHALE FALL

So, a whale dies and sinks down into the dark —
a hundred and fifty tonne lipid sack
scrawling an uneven *Z* as it falls.
It's going down wearing its original skin,
taut to near-split from gasses put off
by the decompositional stink
getting its brew on inside.

Near the belly of the whale
a smell so strong it engages the third eye.
An awakening easily mistaken for headache.

The whale's plunging towards the plane
that underscores the edge of ocean-zone
named for midnight. It meets the deep-sea earth,
and even half-pickled, the smell alights in
the skulls of scavengers, calls them out
of the oily smear of saline.

Hagfish writhe like apoplectic tongues,
gnaw on flesh through grinding plates.
Crumbs of soft tissue abandon the frenzy
and embed in the sea floor. Worms crop up
from the sediment like phantom grass.

What scaffolding's left is bandaged
with bacteria: a whale skeleton draped
in a polar bear's skin. If anything
could be etched here, make some claim
on light's glance, it would be this.
But it can't.

Because this is one way the earth ends:
abyssal, superlative with all-dark,
an absence too thorough
to be imagined in a living body.
Darkness that registers as gravity,
gives weight to anything with mass.

A SHORT HISTORY OF THE VISIBLE

If we were all laid prone, stiff, still the sky would be experimenting with its blues and its golds. — Virginia Woolf

*

Look at the view:
it's like a Magic Eye.

And if you could just flex your focus a little softer,
convince the part of you that's pressed
against the membrane of your pupil's porthole
to ease up, you could probably see
something good in it.

*

Silver clutters in on itself.
Skating over celluloid to mark
in layers all the places, earlier,
where light wasn't.

*

The Great Wall of China
isn't visible
from space.

*

Cameras make everything
beautiful for a while.

Out-of-frame is ground down
into myth. Netting flushes there
like a paisley of hives under skin,
shining like a corrosive, lovely weed.

It's so lightly barbed it seems
only sticky. A fine-grained darkness
is caught up in it and never identified,
though a science is invented
to document the attempt.

*

The earth moves
beneath the plane
of the pendulum swinging.

The pendulum measures rotation
relative to some unknown thing.

Don't you believe me?

*

Glass. It's important to mention glass.

*

There is a mountain range in Iceland
in which beams of igneous rock
are threaded with human hair.

That no one has yet discovered this
has no bearing on the fact
that it's true.

*

Body scanners once used only in airports
become popular in bars.

This is what you see:
clothes haunting skin haunting
muscle haunting bone.

What you see is what you get.

*

The view doesn't need you.

It doesn't need your coaxing or your soft focus.
It doesn't need you to give it some space.

Without you, it will still bloat
into a third dimension and reveal
a looming tiger's head, sunflower, sailboat —
whatever meaning comes reeling out of it.

SOME CRUCIAL ELEMENT

A SHORT AND USEFUL GUIDE TO LIVING IN THE WORLD

Take, say, the roster of details worried into a day
like grit in unlaundered wool:

>Bridge, spinal-thin, trellised across
tracks to keep you presiding over
some take on a city's spread

>Mottled wet of early morning's
pavement oily, slick as an animal
hide

>Paper jammed in the outbound
roller tray, inking out strains
like an overnight drift off
unwashed eyelashes

>Staircases laced with violated
building codes

Re-camp these entries along new lines,
unearth the alliances between them.
There is much work to be done, each instant
cleft open like a horizontal fluke.

Spend time loitering, slipping coins into attention's slots,
anticipating the next big payoff.

When you tire of this, you can mouth a word
until the seam of its meaning splits open.
(Try *goulash*. Try *transmogrify*.)

Ask or be asked: *which way does the ballerina spin?*
Use your hours trying to catch the image on its axis,
shadow flipping over shadow, and think to yourself:
you'll dizzy your senses on all the things you didn't choose.

The trick is to try to live in Earth time
and keep the vigil of an orbit around anything.

Employ these and other strategies that prove useful.

Please write to me of your success.

SEASONAL GOODS

One season, I caught a rat under a recycling bin
and waited for letters. This became less an activity

and more a solid thing activities play out against,
like built-in storage units, or a trampoline flush

with the floor, or even a long, quiet pipeline riffing
some crucial element from nowhere special

to somewhere else. My memory of this time
looks like a demo reel coaxed from cutting room

floor-scraps of an unfunded mumblecore flick.
The urge to package events by their season

is strong. Someone told me recently that a country
should be what you can drive across in a day.

When I went to see the place the letters came from,
I spent three days watching scenery trill past

windows wide as bedsheets, like stock footage
overriding a green screen to offer proof of motion.

I arrived in patio season. The sun regularly
outstayed what I considered its welcome.

A cluster of coincidences had hooked in me
like the barbed end of a taser, convinced me

to cross the ungainly country in the first place.
I'll admit, I was looking to feel synchronicity

blooming underfoot like a small rampage
of low-grade earthquakes, and my instrument

for measuring inevitability was probably
more sensitive than it needed to be.

I took a different landlocked route home,
but the view was the same.

BRACKETING PARADOX

It's like if you took a way of thinking
and divided it by two, until it wasn't thinking
but a thought itself. It's like if you took something
you were already thinking (the kind of thinking
that's so familiar it barely registers as thought)
and put it back on the shelf where it belongs.
It's like if you hung a shelf overtop of a thought,
secured it firmly in the studs that bear in against,
or bear up, or just bear to be near the wall.
It's like if your thought had already happened
and even though it seemed familiar you registered
it in an online directory and built a dollhouse
for it to live in. It's like if you had a thought
that grew too large for its quarters, too much
to bear up, and it neededto move out, find a job,
look for real estate, start putting itself out there,
stop putting things on hold. It's like a kind of thinking
that divides itself in two until it's not an activity
but a thought that's formed, that is a form,
and it's two nouns strung together, and it's a device
(or is it supposed to be a person?) that can hold on,
hold you still (you in particular, you more than anyone),
hold you tight, hold you where you are, bear in against,
bear up, or just bear to be there, near you, keeping
you intact, keeping you upright, keeping you
as you are, and as you have been, and as you will be.

FUN WITH COUNTERFACTUAL CONDITIONALS!

Match Antecedents in Column A with Consequents in Column B

If there hadn't been a condom-thin layer of ice on the road at the bottom of the bridge at the end of April

If you'd invested in real estate

If you'd had a taste for spicy foods

If you'd drunk a box of wine

If you'd mentioned that when you were seventeen you'd unsuccessfully attempted to hang yourself

If there'd been a tree well suited to a rope outside the cafeteria at the camp for poor kids from fucked-up families where you worked

If you hadn't invested in real estate

If you'd been a driver

If you'd been a drinker

If you'd owned a dog as a child

If your talent for dance had been recognized and nourished

then you would have developed the nervous habit of prodding at your arm with your index finger as though testing for a sunburn.

then you would have had better core strength.

then you would have cultivated several unshakeable convictions.

then you would have entered a period of sustained personal and financial security.

then you would have forgotten yourself.

then you'd have forgotten that your interlocutor was the same person to whom you'd once lost your virginity.

then the person to whom you lost your virginity would have abstained from fucking anyone for several years in early adulthood.

then you would have kept at it.

then you would have forgiven yourself.

then the brakes would have had something to cultivate a little friction with.

POSITION: MONSTER

found poem

Job Description:
Enhance each guest's enjoyment of a maze
by scaring them as they travel through the maze,
while providing the highest possible
standard of guest service.

Job Requirements:
Able to work outside in a variety of weather conditions,
able to stand for an extended period of time,
able to work in dark, confined spaces with loud noise,
able to work in fog/haze/strobe lighting,
able to wear a latex mask for prolonged periods of time,
dependable and enjoy working in a guest-oriented team-based environment.

NOTES TOWARDS SOMETHING NEARLY ALLEGORICAL ALSO

You're in it: umbilical building reaching towards the day's membrane,
a thin container of amniotic sky.

You're rising, looking out onto a spread of city that pivots on its own logic,
a compulsive Rubik's cube flicker shifting nearer a more reasoned end.

Still and standing, you're letting leverage go through the motions
that vehicle your winging upward, box-bound, untoward.

Aiming from everywhere, light passes through whatever it can,
sifting particles to say with authority what is solid.

The lines below won't tell you much as you try to intuit
which directions will cleave, cardinal, and move the magnet of you.

Glass never forgets how it began: viscous, easily blown open.

CONFESSIONS FROM THE DRIVER OF THE GOOGLE STREET VIEW CAR

The mid-leveller who trained a fleet of us
said that this would be a map on steroids.
The technology is the art-of-the-state.
The camera you'll be equipped with is all-seeing.

I thought about all-terrain, tires the size
of Olympic gymnasts cartwheeling
under me, grips nunchuking up hunks
of dirt where I'd go roadless.

Alright, so, it's not like that.
But it is the kind of gig you get used to.
Benefits. A chance to travel,
if travelling is the sort of thing you go for.

Truth is, it's a butter dish they've got me wheeling in —
but that nine-sided eye-on-a-rod shafted
up on top has something going for it.

People pay attention.
They duck and cover at the sight of me,
point fingers, flip birds, wave flags,
hold up whatever they've got their hands on.

People get their hands on all kinds of things.
I don't even mind.
I sort of like it when they gawk.

Often, though, I drive past someone
who doesn't notice me at all, doesn't know
they'll wind up frozen mid-motion

in a play-by-play of whatever dumb day
they're parading towards.

In the end, it won't be them, exactly.
(*Privacy protection is paramount*, they told us.)
A computer fixes each pedestrian face
into a pixillated hash.
You might not even know yourself.

So, where do you live?
I've driven lots of places.

CHANGE OF STATE

Every door you've tried has *Occupied*
warming in its midriff like an infected tattoo.

A banjo track will spank anything with good cheer.

Colourization technology really
dials up film noir.

Address your problems with the insectlike
industry of a NASCAR pit stop.

Fifteen seconds, and you'll be good to go
around in circles.

RAPTURE BEGETS SWEATER BEGETS RAPTURE

Despite its name, the "sweater curse" is treated in knitting literature not as a superstition governed by paranormal forces, but rather as a real-world pitfall of knitting that has real-world explanations and solutions.
— *"The Sweater Curse," Wikipedia*

The Rapture Index is by no means meant to predict the rapture, however, the index is designed to measure the type of activity that could act as a precursor to the rapture. — *Raptureready.com*

We spent all summer sucking face,
camped out in eddies of green knotted into
downtown's monument-grey warp-and-weave,
tourists nearby snap-shooting
their best faces into place.

We didn't have much to do. We kept busy
reaching out to one another like the body
is a problem worth getting to the bottom of.

The days were hot and amphibious: air seemed
as easy to drink as it was to breathe.
Wherever we were going, we arrived
half-sun-stroked, frail cotton clothes
soaked through. It's weird how lips don't sweat.

It was too hot to say the word *wool*.
I knit for you in secret, at night, while the asphalt
threw back the day's catch of heat. My needles
kept splicing strands, stitches clawing over
one another as though fighting for survival
in a primordial stink, multiplying like cells.

That summer it was all about the End Times.
Everyone was talking about the Rapture Index.
The churches kept tabs, and the tally ran high.
They were crunching numbers, studying signs,
guessing what the world's curtain line would be.

All that weather: tsunamis, hurricanes,
the sky like frosted glass from ash sent up
by arctic volcanoes. (Core-shaken, hurling up
my molten insides, I related to the latter.)

Starlings fell from the skies in the Midwest,
wet and deliberate, landing like they'd been
chucked there by a pitching machine.

Don't forget the economy and all its failures,
slip-ups greasy as the continent of oil
that flooded a whole gulf's meniscus.

Should we have taken the prophecies to heart?
Probably. But our own rapture was more pressing.
The newspapers and the radio hummed,
but you and I had a lot of making out to do.
Remember, too, that I was addled
from a lack of sleep: my vision often doubled,
and I saw two of you.

The prophets had promised fire, but there was only light
so strong it made a sound, a high thrumming
in the chopstick-thin bones in my hands.

The light was encouraging. It bred excess,
the smallest things spawning fastest.
A mat of bacteria unfurled over lawns

and sidewalks, licked the edges of buildings
the off-white colour of someone's sick tongue.
I saw a mouse the size of a beach ball
wade into the river and swim away.

Hair became a skein overnight,
strangled the first casualties in their sleep.
Fingers and toes sprung out like divining rods.
Everyone's centre of gravity migrated elsewhere.

The sweater I was knitting spread out
like an old tattoo made awry by weight gain.

I thought that I would have something new to say
about all of it. Or about anything, really,
but the light cleaved spaces between things,
pushed my thoughts apart like venetian blinds
turning outward. I couldn't even remember your name.

Time slowed like a game show wheel ticking down,
each moment lingering a little longer, threatening
to be the last stop.
No one could say when the sun had last set.
One long day spread like a bleeding stain.

So, this is how the world ends:
by not ending at all.

There is only more and more
and more of what we already have.

I knit like it could conjure a heartbeat.
I didn't count. I couldn't see the end.

KEEN FREQUENCIES

I LIKED THE PART WHERE

This is the part with the compelling opening sequence, where there is movement, and a landscape, possibly even movement across a landscape.

This is the part with the bus or train, maybe a window, someone looking out of it.

This is the part with the arrival in weather, and the weather is evocative of something.

This is the part with a beginning, the part where you lie in bed and wait for a reason to begin.

This is the part where you think about how no one knows you're awake, and you wonder if you even are awake, and you wonder what counts.

This is the part where you don't dress properly for the weather.

This is the part where you press the wrong button on the elevator, and then realize your mistake and press the right one, and after you've gotten off, the elevator travels up an extra floor for no reason.

This is the part where you avoid saying someone's name because you worry you'll mispronounce it or that what you think is their name maybe isn't their name at all.

This is the part where you yawn so wide your jaw dislocates and gets stuck open.

This is the part where you change your Facebook status to a list of nouns that appeal to the senses in an effort to somehow give the impression that you are living your life to its fullest.

This is the part where you don't quite hear what someone's just said, so you laugh and say, "Yeah, for sure," and hope you'll come across as generally amiable or something.

This is the part with a montage of time passing that makes time passing look pretty great.

This is the part where you try to think of one good thing.

This is the part where there's been too much of a good thing.

This is the part where it's the best of all possible worlds.

This is the part where the simplest answer is the most likely.

This is the part where everything that's already happened happens again.

This is the part where nothing happens.

This is the part where nothing.

DREAD FOR SOMETHING USEFUL

Let's think about the desert.

If I had to bet, I'd say every part
of a kingdom has its scavengers.

A light sadness is like ice jostling
for space in a glass, getting comfortable,
learning to love itself just as it changes
into something else.

We both court a haunting.

So, you make a playlist called Bleak House
and set it out as bait.

I prefer the tactic of being prone,
lying on familiar surfaces in declining
weather, grubbing for warnings.

A short squall of foreign place names
can be soothing as a parabola.

Repetition is the spice of melancholy.

There's a texture in the air around me
I'm always trying to reach through.
The threat of touching
what's beyond it looms large.

You tell me to use that dread
for something useful.

You wouldn't understand.

You pocket dial me, and I push my
ear to the back-loaded static, trying to find
the moment two estranged dialects make
themselves understood to one another.
It's like feeling for the end on a roll of tape.

Try me.

SOME FINAL EXPLANATORY THOUGHTS

after Samantha Li

Okay, so in the beginning we're running,
and there's a sense of a lack of destination.

The person I'm with has this resistant quality —
a tendency to make categorical statements
about how things really are.
That's how I know it's you.

There's some kind of hybrid human being held aloft.
We're fleeing from some people or force
that demands we consider it good.
We're meant to be struck with wonder.

(There are these strange connotations
of hailing and accepting a husband
in some kind of marriage-market situation.)

Every time I begin to doubt the purpose
of our resistance, there's your reassertion
that we must —
       You know, the whole thing feels like a scene
       out of *The Island of Dr. Moreau*
       (the bad movie, not the book).

In the end, the hybrid thing is like a calf strung in wire,
and we're pelting it with small bags of carrots.
It's dying because we refused to validate it
in the way we were expected to.

But there's no sense that resisting
or not resisting
was the right thing after all.

There's something equally horrific about running
as there is about pelting carrots at the calf.

KEEP SCROLLING

A three-legged dog chasing down a ball,
pumping forward like a skier going over moguls . . .

burnt calcium, knots where rocks
erode a river, time-lapse photograph
of fireflies, misguided vacation purchase . . .

triptych of Nicolas Cage portraits
on black velvet, a model of
Euro Disney made to scale . . .

dinosaur-going-on-fish with tarp-thick flesh
held in by a strangely delicate exoskeleton . . .

glass vase that mimics a trumpet,
houses breaking ground like baby teeth,
badminton birdies beaming their heads
back the way they came . . .

something that looks audible but isn't,
a traffic island no one visits,
hares the size of dogs, teeth
cut with an otherworldly meanness . . .

and so on
and so forth . . .

GOOD THING

The sky's an homage to planned obsolescence.
It's rocking a case of feature creep, clouds

like drool blooms filling a pillow faster
than you can say: *Careful or your face*

might get stuck that way. This cloud leans in
like an unfinished limb activating a bus door.

This cloud's a lab rat acing the swim test.
The edge of the light is like sweet, panic-thick

hand soap. If this is emergency, I'm digging
the time-delay function. Don't mind if I stay

on the line while last decade's chart-toppers
put me back in touch with some crescendos

I'd lost track of. As for my own face, I'm just
a little worried about the aperture that lets

amazement in. Good thing I have an insider
view of the weather. Good thing I'm in a mood

to appraise. This rain's a spread of plot points
jonesing for the line that fits best.

The day's a round of Edward Fortyhands,
and I've fallen behind. Whenever I think

it might be time to cut out, get my jollies
another way, some new element checks in,

like an almost-not-mechanical voice: *You're important. Please stay. Someone will be with you.*

ONE POSSIBLE EXPLANATION FOR WHAT APPEARS TO BE THE CASE

It's true no one used the word *good* to describe it, never said
it would resonate with our higher-order selves,
or, failing that, be subject to an order of operations,

or operate under the influence of some kind of beauty,
thumb the nodes that make our insides look like dashboards.
And now that I reflect on it, maybe it was implied we should

sponge at certain corners of our vocabulary, ply a trade
with diligence, look for a good tailor of expectations,
dial down any keen frequencies we might be tempted

to listen in on. Still, words like *good* and *beauty* frequent
the same bars as I do, turn up like a colour haunting the primer
laid down over it. And you know, I'm pretty sure no one

said I would need to spend so much time lying down
and thinking about permafrost, or anything about the indifferent
means of travel, all the elsewhere failing to catch and ignite.

I've heard there's something catching going around that might
explain a few things — for example, this feeling that inside my body
there's a roll of film threatening to open and unfurl in a hurry,

or the rolling deadline we keep setting for the apocalypse. All that
could be some kind of reverse-fever talking. And maybe there's still
reason to hope for an arrival, or a standing invitation somewhere.

So, that's why I'm standing here like some chump on an anthill
holding a saw by the wrong end, dowsing for meaning.
Just waiting for all the wild nodding to begin.

NOTES ON THE POEMS

"Thirteen Subcategories" were, at one time, the subcategories filed under "Accidental Death" on Wikipedia.

"Already Today You Have Had Several Very Good Ideas" contains lines from an interview by WNYC's *Radiolab* with composer William Basinski. The poem's overall structure is a loaner from Kevin Connolly.

"Portraits of Several Lamps Broken While House-Sitting" is for Gil Adamson and Kevin Connolly.

"I Wish You Luck and Prosperity!" contains wording inspired by real chain letters, available online in The Paper Chain Letter Archive.

"The Windsor Asylum" is for Madeleine Cohen, Elisabeth Oakham, and Rosanna Nicol.

The opening line of "Whale Fall" is taken from a *Radiolab* interview with oceanographer Craig Smith, and many of the poem's images are lifted from the same interview.

The epigraph to "A Short History of the Visible" comes from Virginia Woolf's essay "On Being Ill." The first line of the poem is a variation of a repeated phrase from Woolf's *Between the Acts*. A section of the poem refers to Foucault's pendulum as explained by Professor Jim Labelle on YouTube.

"Position: Monster" comes from a recent Canada's Wonderland job ad sent to me by Molly Lynch.

"Dread for Something Useful" is for Andrew F. Sullivan.

Most of "Some Final Explanatory Thoughts" is taken from an email sent to me by Samantha Li, whose tragic death in 2009 took away a lovely human with a brilliant mind.

ACKNOWLEDGEMENTS

Earlier versions of some of these poems appeared in *CV2*, *Dragnet Magazine*, *Forget Magazine*, *Joyland Poetry*, *Matrix*, *The Puritan*, *The Walrus*, and in the anthologies *Desperately Seeking Susans* (Oolichan) and *The Puritan Compendium I* (The Puritan). A selection of these poems was published as the chapbook *Sucks to Be You and Other True Taunts* (Odourless Press). Several other pieces were contained in a nomination for the RBC Bronwen Wallace Award for Emerging Writers and published by the Writers' Trust of Canada. Thanks very much to the editors and makers of all these publications. Bonus thanks go to Bardia Sinaee at Odourless Press for his canny edit and design, and to Michael Lista at *The Walrus* for passing my name on to ECW.

I'd like to acknowledge the Toronto Arts Council and the Ontario Arts Council for their generous support. I'd also like to super thank the Banff Centre, which is an incredible place.

Thanks to Ken Babstock for being a generous source of wisdom and kind words, Karen Solie for making my time at Banff even more special, and Rosemary Sullivan for support and encouragement. I owe the bulk of this book to Kevin Connolly, whose mentorship has permanently changed the way I write and read. I can't even say how much I appreciate all you people being so nice to me.

Thank you to my Group of Seven and the wider workshop that followed for reading so many of these poems and making them better. Special thanks to Andrew F. Sullivan for faithful commiseration and advice, and to Molly Lynch for a vision and intelligence my own brain could never come up with.

Thank you to my editor, Michael Holmes, for his generous, astute eye, and for making me feel like I could trust myself throughout this process. Thanks also to Emily Schultz for an above-and-beyond copy edit, Natalie Olsen for the cover, and Crissy Calhoun and everyone else at ECW Press for all the things that made this into an actual book.

Thank you to my wonderful family, Peter Showler, Ellen Zweibel, and Adrienne Showler, for all their love and tolerance, and for never filling me in that being a poet is not a real job.

And, obviously, thank you all the time, for all the things, to Andrew Battershill: my first reader, best friend, and only love.

Suzannah Showler's writing has appeared places, including *The Walrus*, *Maisonneuve*, *Hazlitt*, and *Joyland*. She was a finalist for the 2013 RBC Bronwen Wallace Award for Emerging Writers and winner of the 2012 Matrix LitPOP Award for Poetry. This is her first book.